belonging, on self:

poems on dominirican healing

poems by

Cynthia Julissa Roman Cabrera

Finishing Line Press
Georgetown, Kentucky

belonging, on self:

poems on dominirican healing

Copyright © 2024 by Cynthia Julissa Roman Cabrera
ISBN 979-8-88838-434-3 First Edition
All rights reserved under International and Pan-American Copyright Conventions. No part of this book may be reproduced in any manner whatsoever without written permission from the publisher, except in the case of brief quotations embodied in critical articles and reviews.

ACKNOWLEDGMENTS

I want to thank a girl who had a lot of feelings, my inner child, who dreamt this book at age eleven. Te quiero.

Yerrr! A Lesbian Anthem will appear in the forthcoming book Pájaros, lesbianas y Queers...! A volar!

Publisher: Leah Huete de Maines
Editor: Christen Kincaid
Cover Art: Andreina Mijares Cisneros
Author Photo: Shay Sease Photography
Cover Design: Elizabeth Maines McCleavy

Order online: www.finishinglinepress.com
also available on amazon.com

Author inquiries and mail orders:
Finishing Line Press
PO Box 1626
Georgetown, Kentucky 40324
USA

Contents

On the eve of my birth ... 1
Muerte a las paredes ... 2
Paliza ... 3
Greñuda ... 4
Fugue ... 5
Hunger III ... 6
The bakery of brutality ... 9
Hunts Point [5pm] ... 9
El maletín ... 10
Family Heirlooms ... 12
Heart ... 13
Occupy ... 14
Deadass, Pigeons ... 15
Por si acaso me encuentras por ahí: A guide ... 16
Piles ... 17
I carried home in a bag ... 18
Al dedo malo, todo se le pega ... 21
Speculation ... 22
Twenty-year nightmare ... 23
Hunger I ... 25
My body is a bag ... 27
Incarnation ... 28
I opened the window ... 30
A Burial at Sagrada Familia ... 31
Conocer La Niña ... 32
Alba II ... 33
Four poems: Suegra ... 34
Hunger II ... 35

When your visa expires	36
To all the lovers loving from afar	37
La Ciguapa	38
Yerrr! A Lesbian Anthem	40
Traffic in the stars	41
Bittersweet	42
Parenting	43
...and you told me you wanted motherhood	44
Noche Buena / 12.25	45
Big	46
My name is	47

*dedicated to those who yearn something buried, sing soul songs,
who never forgot their tongues were made to sting.*

On the eve of my birth

the wind howled into the night,
pitter-patter green rain
pounded on my chest
I sat with a quiet reserve of power.

Something took hold and
I was beaten furiously
by troubled sticky hands.
I latched onto roots,
wove my tongue to the depths
arms sapped by many.
So, I hitched it to the clouds,
held court and flirted with
grays and floods.
Fashioned my wings of teeth
and word
and stump.

Before long
time behaved—
longing for the spaces
where breath
came easy.
I crawled through my scalp
a quilt of smoothed curls
a being grounded, limitless.

Muerte a las paredes

I will force myself to smile,
to split my grin in two
one for me
the other for a lasting memory.
My anxiety is as old as tracing monsters
out of shapes, lying awake
making the puntitos of the popcorn
ceiling onto bodies of teeth,
the devil lurks in the corner. I stay,
smothered with pounds, slippery with self.
My unconscious is afraid of the spaces.
My heart quickens the tambores in my ears
scared of my own breath,
What does it mean when your inhalation
takes your breath away?
I am limp | *tamarindo seco se le caen las hojas*
my thirst whistles.
walls whimper in my absence.

Source: Tamarindo Seco by Kinito Mendez

Paliza

I hid the correa my mom used to beat me / laid it to be strangled under the bed / for three years before she realized what happened. / But, my thighs stung from the replacement: / a plastic Dominican chancleta. / Once / my mom got so mad / when I rolled my eyes at her / that she slapped my leg with it. / She used her entire arm swing so I could have felt / the tongue and venom sting on my spine / like when you bang your elbow / on that corner and can feel the / concrete race straight to your head? / My mom would hit me so I could forget who I was. / Hit me so I could forget who she was. / Hit me so she can forget who she was. / And so, I stopped crying after I sensed she wanted to hurt me. / My thigh was hot with sting and pattern, / triangular edges on the belly of that chancla / trapezed along my veins, / a stamp of my mother's discipline. I was ten. / Her beatings then became a sort of self / punishment. / My mistakes made me lie down / to watch the whipping of my unconscious. / So if you see my hyper-critical self emerge, / please don't let me drown. / And, if today is overcast / with clouds prickled with rain, / my sadness hides my umbrellas / lingers above my eyes / in a permanent sleep gaze. / Know that I am trying to be better than god / ascending from twenty feet underground / -or last week's high- / too far from this blue. / Let me fall gently into your arms / let me cry those tears she never let me show.

Greñuda

I have always been   hairy
a girl smoothing down
heavy arches that parade my forehead,
lion-tailed macaque, peluda and unrestricted.

Razors grunt and muscle, mow and tame
and all it takes is a gentle breeze to whistle the stands
of strands, a tarantula's shadow prickling and peaking
through denim jeans, a terrible stump
scraping the morning's cacao butter lathering.

There is a provocative filth to hair,
the bushy crawl of it on the cross-Bronx bus floor or
the looming patch in the drain or
the single geometric pattern on a suit:
an exhibitor carcass of its previous life.

But I will never be bald. The shedding maze
silk patterns across my pillow,
the will of *mami, abuela y nena*.

My hair crosses boundaries of comfort, an army spreading
the expansive land of thighs, claiming stretch marks,
muttering an earthly chant of infinite breath
unashamed of this vulgar freedom.

Fugue

All I know is somewhere
between age seven and dark hallways,
I was a *niña buena*,
Afraid to ask for more
than this.
The quiet turned to violence,
space becomes time
so, I don't remember who I was to be,
a life spent weaving the pieces.
Is this a normal state of being?

Hunger III

I have a recurring dream
when I'm hungry,

my stomach twists
and chokes itself.

Food appears and I eat
like a starving pit moaning ecstasy

in dread and despair of it ending,
empty bag ties flapping in the wind.

I chew and spit my slop,
hoping to resuscitate that bite,

saliva mixed with grief, absorbs life
mush newspapers in gray

Again.

and again.

and again.

and again.

The wet decay returns to my mouth
as I search for the flavor in fervor,

Never again,
like a fiend itching for a fix.

So now, I buy groceries, jingling
the change in my pocket,

a carajita with opportunity
to eat and see food in the fridge.

I stack and display the cans, tomatoes, bread, salami, rice
a shrine

to my growling stomach, an offering for calm
I bow to myself in thanks.

I trick and fool my stomach, with prendas shining
in temporary relief, though calamity always wins.
I am a broken record of want.

The bakery of brutality

*Free all the
homies*

A blue belt is hung,
metal buckle clinks
shadows, weave baskets
bulging with deceit,
and fickle beasts run
buck wild citywide.

Handcuffs be bangin'
black and blue beatdowns,
see Black mud bound, pound
blistering graveyards
—the dead be bitter.

Pry open the damn
pits! drag dem pasty
boys who dare lay foul
brash moldered bodies
on the innocent.
Let the smoke smolder,
linger at your stoop
oozing shame, bloated
in bloody batons.
Ashes awaken
pale pedestrians!
Paint the mirrors red
demand sacrifices.
Char city's finest.
I beg of you don't
have mercy.

Hunts Point [5pm]

None of these streets have names
none of them have faces—
a blue death beneath eyelids.
Water main breaks
wrinkle and sink
gush through avenues,
street lamps,
gutters and she,
floating above skips of her geese,
feet in flight hears a scratched
record playing
the same rising crescendo,
crescendo
on repeat.

El maletín

To mami

I am here
in my usual place

packed
as I watch her unfold
the false promise
of an american wet dream.

My unpolished leathery skin
gashed from alley fights
with the corner of the closet,
I am her still-life
burdened with duty:
to carry immigration documents,
        birth certificates
       c a s h
no clothing,
no photographs.

She lives on the edge of a fast moving stream,
      not quite drowning,
           towing the line
           with her bare hands,
           waiting for nothing to arrive;
           with me balanced atop her head
           as water reaches above her chin

I — tattoo the trauma of running,
escape a militarized Quisqueya,
stretch my toes through the clasp of my mouth,
raise my voice but fear,
for my metal knees buck and beg her to stop running
desperate not to scream,
tickling her fingertips to remember;
her secrets shake me quiet, erasing
the memory of the chains
of her people.

She is in a constant
state of running
and though we have never ran away,
she's never really unpacked,
at any moment
we can be gone

Source: Sonia Sanchez "I've been a woman"

Family Heirlooms

The whole world took
several seats,
clutched her pearls,
her leaky gas pipelines.
Burned all the plastic enriched rice.
Threw down,
and gave up.

*****

Lockdowns are like unemployment lines
each head dunking the last
just to get a glimpse, a licked corner
of crumbs of those with choice.
Communal living requires control,
but the bills double at our stagnancy.

Abusers do not get to defend
themselves.
pass down the line fatigue laced in arrogance
Violent stories morphed into immigrant pain
serves for excellent admissions essays.

We check ourselves on the bodega window
pass down vanity.
There is luxury
in preserving
a person's essence.

So I buy my little sister a tiny jewelry box,
we may be something
someday.

Heart

To long distance, the third wheel

I live in a disarray of pounding.
I can hear my heart running.
The hollow swallows my vision
and I speak only in carnage.
My mouth fails to speak the memory of love
but this little light of ours,
I will not let it dim.
The neighbors will eat our words
and my ears will beep with silence
as if my fury bounced the walls deaf.
I am afraid you will leave.
When did we last argue without panting with pain?
Your impatience shouts in a hurry,
combusts.
I can be cruel with honesty
Some people cannot handle the mirrors.
My heart speaks before humility can take the wheel.

Occupy

To da fam

I walk on the sunny side of the road
our hands are phantoms
of Brown faded buildings,
stiff necks broke the memory of home
in blue gold etched anthora cups,
baconeggandcheeses.
Ma of conscious selection.

America takes over tongues.
I must have missed the memo.

Deadass, Pigeons

Nine
filed high
hung against a perfect
blue sky,
a firing squad
order, a Broadway
cancan—
horizon of tombs.
Telephone lines
criss-cross, dangling
a set of Js, hanging
a prophet's final resting place.
Oh pigeons,
bow to the look-outs
of the bodega heist;
secret-keeper, turning
an all-knowing eye to word,
shitting anointment
on that interview blazer.
We are not the same.

Por si acaso me encuentras por ahí: A guide

1. I always carry my ID in case my body is found in a ditch—this body is a carcass of catcallers and bruised egos

2. My favorite time of day is right after I eat when the underside of my belly has settled its contents

3. I peel first, then the second layer of orange so each bite is equally as sweet

    My friends are all extensions of my future selves

4. If you're tall, you will awkwardly watch me push my glasses up with my nose to really see you

5. On moonlit nights, boleros take me by the hand and sway me *ba da da da ba* across cracked sidewalks

6. Most often I'm judging you—carajo I get it de mami

    Anxiety grinds my teeth at night, the dust of my head blots my dreams. Maybe that's why I'm blind in my sleep

7. My sadness is a needy bitch, a child calling for help—or maybe a hug—a trauma from long ago, to be listened to, understood, seen, cared for, spoiled, enjoyed

Piles

Home,
heaps of
clothes
gaze guilty
knowing
lumps
grow
legs,
cave
upwards
on our bed
pressing
onto
your
toes
they
wiggle
worry,
havoc
grooms
home.

Not touching your stuff.

I carried home in a bag

the bright fluorescent light,
casts the room white,
pales the bobbing heads
of my siblings, violent in sleep.
the shelter swallows us,
including mami.
y dónde está mami?
snow covers
car hoods
our black bags
trssssst
        trssssst
across the slushy pavement,
noise amplifies the sleep-deaf ears.
black bags
puffy coats
puffy eyes
heavy in sleep and ice.

the cheese finally bus pulls up,
bitter fall air gnaws
our fingernails,
raw with detail
       graffiti trains
       sparks of splintering shit.
as we shuffle our heavy bags,
disguised as strangers' belongings,
landing our asses on green plastic seats
poking at our resistance
cold
hard
invasive.

the yellow street lamp offers veil service
to the black bags seemingly light in
yellow light,
yellow
yellow bus blinding
flashing light.

**

we step into a harlem shelter,
the city different when home
pounds the toes cold.
the doors are projects brown,
bodies picked and sorted
into rooms, and we climb the stairs
onto a third-floor brick winter.
one by one we crawl onto cold
blankets—stale dust, cigarettes, yellow
streetlamp tucks us to slumber.
my sister at the bottom, me on the top bunk,
my brother already gone y la
plays tag with her sleep.
coat and boots laced up, tight.
mami is nowhere.
lullabies shiver with sleep
into the longest shortest night,
black bags rest, unhook after a long day

footsteps approach,
thunder in hurry
too
early,
I am
am
am so cold,
cold.
they pound on doors.
homelessness is never tardy.
mamiiiiii
black bags slung over droopy shoulders,
eye bags run away the stiff cold.

we board the bus towards
fluorescent lights and tired mothers

light so bright
closed eyes see yolky yellow,
green edges
reflect on
orange eyelids.
fast blink,
blink
blinking light away
only to find the light swells
your eyeballs into hazy circles,
blink haze
broken looking glass.
i am afraid.
responsible for the four of us.
my shivers are a reminder that I am here
so, I follow the shadow of sleep to
the cold tiled floors, find a body
awaken the light.
and ask the moon
why she sleeps,
as the dust settles
the grind gears of my jaw.
i scratch at the cold,
and moan for release

Al dedo malo, todo se le pega

Seven years lost
        unhinged composure
Seven years numb
        nervous
phone calls hold their breath
portraits disappear
my name is silence
Seven years blend
        six
Seven years swallowed
        idle stumble
        houses wish
echo memory
Seven years
        una hija sin rostro
Seven years smolder
alive and beefin'
        petty
Seven years blend
        nine
Seven years twirls a braid
        resign
Seven years
forget
years forg
ive
        released
Seven years cursed.

Speculation

In a previous life, we would have walked into the nearest bodega
yanked the cords from the walls
the *skrrr* interrupts another spineless bachatero,
and we'd wrapped his arms to the chips display.
Bags would rain on his chest, the same way dread
pulled onto yours when he could not resist not minding his business.
You would be unafraid to rock your sexy,
your cheeks would be strapped with latex,
every dimple flirting with the day,
cheeks squeeze together like s'mores,
except, the drip would be entirely organic.
Your nails would pinch the soft cushions of his neck,
veins running with fear, prickly,
fill a million goosebumps.
You could hold tight, see how far your anger could take you.
The body adjusts fate.

> Instead you hang your head, walked a little faster
> freeze the sway in your thighs and pretend to be a stick,
> unmemorable, flawed, aged.
> In a previous life, we would fill our mouths
> with sweet chocolate pound cakes,
> hunt the taste within each of us

Twenty-year nightmare

To the cuco within me who haunts my dreams

The darkness stings
pupils, pulsing black

bees scratching white, grainy
murk sending static

flashes in my eyes.
Steps echo in my ears,

a chapel of heels
bouncing off the walls

of our narrow hall
way. Pressing my face,

*pushing the door
back so the hinges cry out,*

*devils, their thumbs crushed,
their pointed noses tweezed.*

The devil does not sleep,
cradles my head, plucks

hair strands for voodoo.
A shadow lurks behind lashes,

a figure eclipses dawn,
the hole in my living room.

Table.
Couch.

Television
becoming an entire world and

the walls red in slick lungs
never getting through.
But once, running,

blindly past the living room
to the hallway, figure teetering

on my shoulders
swallowing hall space.

**

Awake, cowering in
breath, heart beats drive

to madness. Loosen the grinding
bones of my teeth, dust off the window

of shadow, to die mornings,
clavicle caverns mourn.

Source: Julia Alvarez: How the Garcia Girls Lost their Accents

Hunger I

To welfare

This morning, I screamed
into the green,
empty pockets of my jeans.
Eyes wide shut,
curtains of blue
forced open with fans
windy in nails and dust.
Mornings yearn structure,
the white of diplomas
weaves solitary webs
in stored boxes.
It costs more to be without.

How many degrees to be fed?
How many languages to be considered?
How many years of experience?

This should be the end of this misery.
The agony of guessing next meals, watching
the world pass me by, a busy anonymous
insect nipping at my ears.
My stomach growls.
Constantly,
consecrated pupils watch the rush of time.
Another paycheck gone.
Nevertheless robbed and stolen and yanked
by classism, tongue and chow.

I've done my best in this zip code.

And the last,
    At last
I want to shed my skin,
start anew,
color myself in pollen
like the mink on coat
be the feed for the air.

Let soliloquy drip on walls
to distract me from my inbox of bills,
dance on the crack of cement floors.

Peak the green of a salary on the horizon,
to crawl myself into a seated position,
plea and bleed for another day to survive.
I'm hungry.I'm hungry.I'm hungry. I'm hungry.I'm hungry.I'm hungry.I'm hungry.I'm hungry. I'm hungry.I'm hungry.I'm hungry.I'm hungry.I'm hungry. I'm hungry.I'm hungry.
                                                  when I could not be.

My choice to live another life should not be a death wish.
To crave another world should not be a trap.
To desire an existence outside the monotony.
To have a choice where my family is created.
But I am hungry for life right now.

My body is a bag

the eve of my limbs are weary,
a bag of colorful spheres
clipping and banging,
morphing the pallet in
schemes of a daily grunge of
walking by peering eyes.
the men's slobber forms puddles
beneath my toes.
My chest begins to expand,
constrict
squeeze
shrink
e x p a n d
shrink
squeeze
my body,
a bubble where breath,
constricts with transparent light;
a prisoner to words.
water in my lungs, bones
lodged in my throat,
sinking between marrow,
water in my cheeks,
an expulsion of teeth.
My eyeballs soak
in the shadows tell me to
sheet my vision,
this shall pass.
just as eyelids move to
hide masks of woe

Incarnation

I exhale dust,
cough up a few bugs
and spit stiff pages,
in this breathing novel;
an index of birthdays.
Letters stamp stride,
trail ellipses...
questions
mark
a hanging—
on the lobes of my ears.

My breath a fluttering flip of fine pages,
fleeting photographs of this angst inferno.
Pages lift like the swing of curls,
swept by gusts of a peanut
scented air. My body
sturdy,
straight,
strong,
carve the edge of a spine—
branded by strange men's copyright,
cattle prodded by waterproof
librarian hands.
I sport this leather skin with the wear
and tear of that spent spine.

Laughter, the adjectives that conduct
music from my *very* still life,
lovers wish to stay within the fire
of my pages, to never be lost
discovering contents of the next page,
to feel, to visualize
without consequence.

The hum of opening my eyes,
not yet weary with dread,
abstracts on the folds of a woman's

worried lines, tracing tragedy
down to her depressor septi
disguised to lovers
as favorite parts of her body.

I opened the window

To an evening in Barcelona

and the breeze comes in like a tidal wave colliding with the room. All the doors slam in a huff, bring the mountain and worm after storm. Moon light smudges my pupils, chases my peeling arched back. The wind presses against my collarbone, making bugs of my baby hairs, fools with the weedy curly tumbles under the bed. I have never been here. My bed, amongst the mountain and beach, floats to the stars. The night is clear. My city is not made of clarity. I surrender to this night, align my breath to the wisps between my fingertips.

A Burial at Sagrada Familia

Cuando yo muera my arms will kick to the curb these leafy columns
this death will be of grandness of the goddess.
Do not close my eyes for they have seen man,
I will drag in cigarette buds—me inventaré a pillow
and carry the black of silhouette to cushion the corners,
as if death were not enough, my marrow [has carried] a bruise.

My eyes will weep onto steamy manholes,
the gum-spotted sidewalks will design my altar.
and all my wishes will stain glass my cheeks.
I will crawl myself this roof,
spend decades fashioning each prenda
on my passion façade, porque Mami supo:
if you want something done, do it yourself.

This will be a needy death since these walls absorb
the pains of life—I want no more to feel.
Sharpen my eyeliner, master every edge
summon an echo ceremony of my lungs.
These greñas will carry me home.

Source: Sing, Unburied, Sing

Conocer La Niña

When I was five years old, I saw my mom faint on the block by the dome. And I couldn't do anything. When I was 7 papi choked mami and broke me and my sister's childhood bureau, fist clenched in the denial of his anger. My body shook with fear and anger and I forgot to be a child. I was scared of him. His voice thundered through leaf thin walls. The hallway to my parent's bedroom became the obstacle of finding that child again. At 14, I learned my dad wasn't really my father, the fog of those years a remembrance of why I wasn't truly their child. My skin was too pale, and my foot was too far out the door to be that child again. I was 9 and 13 and 16 and 18 when mami pushed me away with her predictions of leaving and never returning. She was right. I wanted me out because she wanted me out. Seventeen was when she found out I was dating a Black boy and yelled papi would never walk me down the aisle if I married un negro, un prieto as if she forgot this country grouped us all together. Papi's brown skin was the elephant in my childhood bedroom. And I left my child-like self on her front door. Stepped into 18, in a new state with a mini fridge and my parents in the dust. I was 18 when I chose. Played and laughed again, explored and ran, asked questions unafraid, shared secrets and cried. Molded and shifted to be who I wanted to be. Unafraid of being a fraud in myself because the only person I wanted to be was me. The child that just wanted to be loved and remembered and cared for. I wanted to feel something beyond the hurt of being forgotten. I wanted to be a child again.

Alba II

For my love...

I woke up to the most beautiful sunrise,
rays touched your eyes,
others were on your lips.
It enveloped your hips
and glittered on your skin
making waves of mauve,
sweeping your moles;
the sun caressed your stretch marks,
like desert sand
cocooning your thighs in light
shadowing the rest.
The sun wakes you with goosebumps
to part your lips in welcome
of another moment of life
together

Four poems: Suegra

IV: Tone deaf

The user you are trying
to reach
is unavailable.
Please try again later.

III. Absent

She spends all day scrolling but, avoids the messages
life comes in the shapes of fifteen-second flashes
I chill out in the gaps with impatient
pause. Flood displeasure's pages.

II: Offline

Neglected double blue check marks
are coordinates of her pain,
gnawing monsters illuminating
her failures of motherhood.

I. Aloof

Put it on mute, stick my head underwater
better to clog up the tubes than intent avoidance
or even asking, even boundaries.
Let's haunt the trivial.

Hunger II

To apartment living in 2019

Quiet hunger storms the rooms of my body,

lingers with the lonely smell of the empty refrigerator,

musky, it wanders across

my grumbling stomach, sorry it even spoke.

My eyes are red with want and everything is edible:

peeling paint

moldy onions

the notes behind my ears.

I cry to fill myself, to forget the fatigue of searching.

To ransack my dreams would be too easy.

my nightmares block the gates and laugh barefoot.

When was the last time I was full?

As I watch, my teeth fall in useless decay.

The rice and beans of

today and yesterday and last week

grin in false promise

of the love I couldn't give to a meal.

When your visa expires

To all the lovers loving from afar

When your visa expires/ I will ask the wind to knock out all the telephone lines/ so that when your mom calls/ she knows you're busy living/ I will design a fake visa/ to make a mockery of the system/ and the walls will peel away with dollar bills/ so you never have to worry again/ about money or paperwork/ the Venezuelan government will just have to wait/ the agents will just have to wait/ because this love is borderless/ when your visa expires/ I will pack up all my things/ erase my footprints/ and follow you to wherever you find peace/ so that we may be together without a timer/ the day your visa ends/ tomorrows will not be counted/ and you can buy yourself that very permanent thing you will never have to carry on a plane/ you will find the time to love without a deadline/ and let go of waiting on visa updates/ when your visa expires it will be morning/ the uncertainty of tomorrow will have passed/ laws will forget borders/ and you will be free/ we will all be free

La Ciguapa

The woman that I am is bitter
mami pulled my hair a lot
so it's not easy to let go.
Children don't mix well with pain.
The steps sometimes disappear
on rotted wood floors,
six flights of stomping,
and still be afraid to make noise.

The woman that I am is
irritated
    irked
        exacerbated
I do not pity ignorant fools.
The center of my body
is the taste of women
losing their minds
a cackle rising from spilled
words bursting into flames.

The center of a woman is brief,
with a gag down my throat
to look in the mirror, gazing
at the truest form of locura,
lurking in the shadows.

The woman that I am is dangerous
una maldita dragging the snarling aching voids,
the crowds of man's imbecility.
Does the moon still feel invited?

This woman is ineffaceable,
an exhaustive pattern of slight.
For me, love is earned not given,
I protect me. This body is a beating
    a blessing.

Yerrr! A Lesbian Anthem

Y es mi lema: ¡ser libre y vivir!
Our feet break them chains.
You will fear me
because my victory will be beautiful

**

Though Quisqueya birthed my forehead
I place no allegiance, but only to the trees.
Don't *aye yo ma! me*
We canceling men cuz they ain't shit,
our letters will no longer be lost.
May the serpent of our tongues drag thee through these streets
and gather only with the forgiveness of time,
We are not asking.
The tremble in our voices is of anger, not fear
so, meet us when our backs stand against themselves
and our gardens water themselves
with the pompa bursting on a Bronx summer afternoon.

Always at the ready with necks held high
our anthem be so loud
the sky calls us home.
The earth dresses us with her flowers,
her streets crown us, mercy,
que templó el heroísmo viril.
Y es mi lema: ser libre y vivir

Holding our power,
because our words save us,
kill us con una fuga dinamita.
But, our letter will not be lost,
cuz we create our own language.
Somos quisqueyanas valientes,
with a yerrr, alcémonos!
Con mighty shield
de ser libre
de ser de aquí y de allá
una comadre amante guerrillera.
De ser libre porque lo merecemos

De ser conciencia lésbica porque queremos
De ser Quisqueyanas valientes porque amamos

que se jodan to'!
we are mighty and free.

Source: Dominican Republic National Anthem

Traffic in the stars

I do not scream,
I grunt. My legs
milky way, twirl a baton
to shimmy off the lace
and hum a bull's cry.
Goddess I will be free,
the want is celestial,
the stars are inside me
so, my legs will be milky,
a traffic jam of moans.
I do not scream,
I howl, a wolf in heat
for the night is my blanket
and my legs are milky
wayward and free,
spotted with light
a dripping cavity.
Because inside is my truth
Because inside is eternity.
I will be milky.

Bittersweet

I left you my scent on the pillow
a pleasure of many tomorrows.
My call will find you there
as you found me when you loved me.

Keep this golden lock of light
to remember that you confide in me,
wrap your fingers around mine
and remind me of the pain of my loss.

Parenting

Last night
I had a dream *que mami*
kissed my fingertips
the same tenderness
breeze has with the flowers.

...and you told me you wanted motherhood

Pa Vane

Your sobs carry the oceans and the loss. Your sobs hold the fatigue of defeat. The
    sirens and the booming could not quiet that quiver on your cheeks.
    Your sobs call for the life of someone, an opaque reflection. The hallway of the building traps your lament, dripping crown molded venom. Walls witness.
    Wallets wheeze destitute, glare at the light. At the sight. Elbow you in recognition of the consequences. Whining water drifts along stiff crumbling couches. You sob onto drying landscapes. I watch with distant dissent your futile dream retreat. Government checks are stingy.
    Your sobs hope. Motherhood is for the adrift grasping at empty promises. It is what it should not be. You were left astray. When bodies exist to be another's food is when the will is lost. Impetus.
    Absence makes the heart decay. Days meander aimless, prophecy got stuck in ghetto traffic. The record player scratches the surface with its neck broken. Your eyes are always searching, never quite landing. The streets pulse with reckoning. A starving mouth.
    Your sobs are a plea for help. Purpose fashioned onto a child is our resigned demise. Our search drowns us everyday. We treasure your sacrifice.
    Your sobs side steps the way. And you told me you wanted a purpose.

Noche Buena / 12.25

The overcast in the sky
takes a lap around my bedroom,
mists under my covers
an empty, foggy road.
The jingle does not merry
and a chariot departs with loud whines.
love does not bother here today.
My robe holds me tightly,
the only touch.
I trifle in thoughts, let it capture me.
There is not a damn thing
to consider
when romance escapes
at any chance.
The mirror aches with reflection,
blame the bitter bark of my banality.
Don't pity the eager melancholic,
who is filled with self deprecating indulgence.
Whip that ass with true compassion
and maybe I can show up
for myself.

Big

I find my voice bounces off the corners of this room, space for the awakening. My skeleton shivers with expectation, a flower bursting with wait. I am no longer a desperate caged bird, the concrete beneath me rips her hat with endless steps. The mornings no longer creak and the empty is just an opportunity to speak. I am breathless with love and awe. It's the bet I thought I'd never win, the one that held joy at arms reach. Now, waiting is just death's call. And I'm no longer standing still. I functioned under limited circumstances—imagine a broken record—a chipped tooth facing broken mirrors. I was that same piranha papi kept in a too small fish tank. I tried to collect the pieces that only felt like a former shell of my bruised body. Pieces that no longer fit into the person I was becoming. The wait is no longer my death. I am not bound by rules. You can no longer take what was already stolen. I am not the puppets with torn strings.

My name is

shapeshifting the edges.
I am the return of some sweltering impact,
the carved blasts of creation,
and extinguished volcanoes
some 3.8 billion years ago.
I am becoming a remote galaxy,
a vast darkness.
Wedging holes in my cheeks,
calcifying the core and opening sores
in the climb through the peaks
wild with green and herstory.
I am beholder of life,
illuminating an everlasting memory,
hangin' with the alien things,
dusting off pockets of footprints,
erasing the water from my belly.
I am the moon,
that little streetlight
guiding a tour through the sky,
I call on the fullness of night,
to etch the shape of my name.

**

My name is celestial and chosen,
penned the sea and blue
the fume of life, designed.

I shall remember me with love, and season
to hear the song that resurrects
to leave me again undone, possessed.

Cynthia J. Roman Cabrera is a Dominican and Puerto Rican native of Brooklyn, New York who grew up in the Bronx and Washington Heights. She is a storyteller, essayist and poet exploring culture and identity, cityscape, familismo, and the healing of her inner child. Her work often uses Spanglish as a literary tool to tell stories on the diasporic challenges of first generation U.S. born people. In her freetime, she nurtures her love of learning and reading in cute bookstores, and chases down any opportunity to satisfy her inner comelona. A trained researcher and evaluator in Public Health, she is energized by tackling complex, systemic social and civic justice issues. She is also a femme person in love. By sharing who she is as a human, she hopes to invite others to break open the writing field with their stories. She has been published in *Brooklyn Poets, changing womxn collective, HerStry, Breadcrumbs, Moko Magazine, Spanglish Voces,* and the *Bronx Magazine*. During the Spring of 2021, Cynthia was named a Brooklyn Poets Fellow. Her forthcoming book, *belonging, on self: poems on dominirican healing*, is her debut collection of poems.

www.ingramcontent.com/pod-product-compliance
Lightning Source LLC
Chambersburg PA
CBHW020343170426
43200CB00006B/489